CLOTHES, COLORS & ACCESSORIES THAT LOOK BEST ON YOU!

A Guide for Teens and Young Adults

UPDATED & EXPANDED

Jennifer Leigh Youngs
co-author of the Smart Teens—Smart Choices series

TEEN TOWN PRESS
www.TeenTownPress.com
info@TeenTownPress.com

www.BettieYoungsBooks.com
info@BettieYoungsBooks.com

Copyright © 2026 Kendahl Brooke Youngs and Jennifer L. Youngs

All rights reserved. No part of this publication may be reproduced, stored in a retrieval system, or transmitted in any form or by any means, electronic, mechanical, photocopying, recording or otherwise, without the written permission of the publisher.

Teen Town Press (www.TeenTownPress.com) is an imprint of Bettie Youngs Books (www.BettieYoungsBooks.com).

Cover by Beau Kimbrel, Kimbrel Designs
Text Design by Beau Kimbrel, Kimbrel Designs
Editorial by Kendahl Brooke Youngs

Available online and from the Ingram Content Group (www.IngramContentGroup.com) and Teen Town Press.

ISBN paper: 978-1-940784-42-7
ISBN eBook: 978-1-940784-43-4

Library of Congress Catalogue Control Number available upon request.

1. Young Adult Nonfiction Literature. 2. Fashion & Style.
3. Self-Image. 4. Appearance, Personal. 5. Scents and Perfume.
6. Smart Shopping Tips. 7. Colors Charts, Personal.
8. Self-Confidence. 9. Body Image

10 9 8 7 6 5 4 3

Distributed by Ingram Content Group (www.ingramcontent.com)

OTHER BOOKS FOR TEENS AND YOUNG ADULTS BY THE AUTHOR

Managing Stress, Pressure, and the Ups and Downs of Life
Information, Encouragement and Inspiration—with commentary by teens
Jennifer Leigh Youngs, A.A. | Bettie B. Youngs, Ph.D., Ed.D.

- Great ways to manage stress and pressure
- How stress works for—and against—you
- Physical, emotional and behavioral signs of stress
- Staying cool under pressure

Book: 978-1-940784-80-9
e-book: 978-1-940784-81-6

Growing Your Confidence and Self-Esteem
Information, Encouragement and Inspirational Short Stories by Teens and Young Adults
Jennifer Leigh Youngs, A.A. | Bettie B. Youngs, Ph.D., Ed.D.

- Being on good terms with YOU
- Feeling "good enough"
- The power of confience
- Liking the face in the mirror
- Being happy and "forward looking"

Book: 978-1-940784-86-1
e-book: 978-1-940784-87-8

Understanding Feelings of Love
Inspirational Short Stories by Teens and Young Adults
Jennifer Leigh Youngs, A.A. | Bettie B. Youngs, Ph.D., Ed.D.

- The lessons of love
- Setting boundaries important to you
- 4 ways to be a great boy/girlfriend
- When love relationships end

Book: 978-1-940784-75-5
e-book: 978-1-940784-74-8

How to be a Good Friend
Information and Encouragement with Inspirational Short Stories by Teens and Young Adults
Jennifer Leigh Youngs, A.A. | Bettie B. Youngs, Ph.D., Ed.D.

- Understanding friendships
- How to be a good friend
- Making, keeping, and ending friendships
- Mending hurt feelings

Book: 978-1-940784-73-1
e-book: 978-1-940784-72-4

Skin, Hair & Nail Care for Teens and Young Adults
Your Total Guide to Beautiful Skin, Hair and Nails
Information, Encouragement and Inspiration—with commentary by teens
Jennifer Leigh Youngs, A.A.

- *How to clean and care for your skin*
- *BEAUTIFUL hair; best styles for you*
- *Choosing soaps and shampoos best for YOU*
- *Grooming your hands, feet, and nails*

Book: 978-1-940784-44-1
e-book: 978-1-940784-45-8

BEST-SELLER!
The Law of Attraction for Teens
How to Get More of the Good Stuff, and Get Rid of the Bad Stuff!
Christopher Combates

- *Improve grades, relationships, and more*
- *Align goals with intentions*
- *Set goals and think positively*
- *Communicate with confidence*

Book: 978-1-936332-29-8
e-book: 978-1-936332-30-4

Faith at Work in Our Lives
Information, Encouragement and Inspirational Short Stories by Teens and Young Adults
Jennifer Leigh Youngs, A.A. | Bettie B. Youngs, Ph.D., Ed.D.

- *Talking faith with your friends*
- *Faith as an anchor in your life*
- *Accepting and caring for others*
- *Faith in victories and defeats*

Book: 978-1-940784-78-6
e-book: 978-1-940784-79-3

How to Be Courageous
Encouragment and Inspirational Short Stories by Teens and Young Adults
Jennifer Leigh Youngs, A.A. | Bettie B. Youngs, Ph.D., Ed.D.

- *The importance of being courageous*
- *The benefits of being brave*
- *How to be a hero*

Book: 978-1-940784-93-9
e-book: 978-1-940784-92-2

Setting and Achieving Goals that Matter to ME
Information and Encouragement for Teens, with Stories by Teens
Jennifer Leigh Youngs, A.A. | Bettie B. Youngs, Ph.D., Ed.D.

- *Discovering what's important TO ME*
- *Hobbies, talents, interests, aptitudes*
- *Hopes, aspirations and dreaming big*
- *My goal-setting workbook*

Book: 978-1-940784-97-7
e-book: 978-1-940784-96-0

How Your Brain Decides If You Will Become Addicted—Or Not
Information and Encouragement for Teens, with Stories by Teens and Young Adults
Jennifer Leigh Youngs, A.A. | Bettie B. Youngs, Ph.D., Ed.D.

- "Using," dependency and addiction
- If you or a friend can't stop using
- Withdrawal, Relapse, and Recovery
- Cool ways to say "no"

Book: 978-1-940784-99-1
e-book: 978-1-940784-98-4

Clothes, Colors & Accessories that Look Best on YOU!
A Guide for Teens and Young Adults
Jennifer Leigh Youngs

- *Choosing Clothes That Compliment YOUR Features*
- *Colors That Make YOU Feel and Look Better*
- *Perfumes That Work For YOUR Body Chemistry*
- *Tips for Being a very SMART shopper*

Book: 978-1-940784-42-7
e-book: 978-1-940784-43-4

The 10 Commandments and the Secret Each One Guards—For You
Information and Inspirational Short Stories
Bettie B. Youngs, Ph.D., Ed.D. | Jennifer Leigh Youngs, A.A.

- How the Commandments speak to you
- The secret each Commandment guards
- Using your faith to guide the choices you make
- How to be confident and bold in your faith

Book: 978-1-940784-95-3
e-book: 978-1-940784-94-6

A Devotional Journal for Teens and Young Adults
Deepen your relationship with God through daily prayer and Scripture.
Jennifer Leigh Youngs, A.A. | Bettie B. Youngs, Ph.D., Ed.D.

- Ask life's big questions
- Connect with God daily
- Grow through weekly devotions
- Reflect with journaling and scripture

Book: 978-1-940784-22-9
e-book: 978-1-940784-24-3

Understanding the Christian Faith
Information, Encouragement and Inspirational Short Stories by Teens and Young Adults
Jennifer Leigh Youngs, A.A. | Bettie B. Youngs, Ph.D., Ed.D.

- 9 Tenants of the Christian Faith
- What is Free Will
- What is the Holly Spirit
- What is "Reap What You Sow"
- How is the Bible as unique from other Holy Books?

Book: 978-1-940784-76-2
e-book: 978-1-940784-77-9

Caring for Your Body's Health and Wellness
Information, Encouragement and Inspirational Short Stories by Teens and Young Adults
Jennifer Leigh Youngs, A.A. | Bettie B. Youngs, Ph.D., Ed.D.

- Food—your body's source of energy
- Sleep—restores body and brain
- Liking the face in the mirror
- Stress, anxiety, and emotional ups and downs

Book: 978-1-940784-88-5
e-book: 978-1-940784-89-2

TEEN TOWN PRESS
www.TeenTownPress.com
info@TeenTownPress.com

www.BettieYoungsBooks.com
info@BettieYoungsBooks.com

AVAILABLE ON-LINE and from the INGRAM BOOK COMPANY

ABOUT THIS BOOK

Clothes, Colors & Accessories that Look Best on <u>You</u>! is for teens and young adults to help you discover your personal style, enhance your appearance, and boost self confidence. It covers topics such as:

- **Appearance and Style:** How your appearance influences others' perceptions, and how to create a personal style that reflects your personality.

- **Wardrobe Organization:** Tips for managing your closet, taking inventory, and identifying what you need to build a versatile wardrobe.

- **Dressing for Your Body Type:** Understanding your body shape and choosing clothes that complement your features.

- **Choosing Colors:** How colors can impact your mood and appearance, and how to identify colors that suit your hair, skin tone, and eyes.

- **Accessories:** How to use jewelry, scarves, and other accessories to enhance your outfits and express your style.

- **Smart Shopping Tips:** How to shop wisely, avoid impulse purchases, and create a wardrobe with versatile pieces that work together.

- **Perfumes and Scents:** The impact of fragrances and how to choose the right scent for your body chemistry, and tips for using perfume effectively.

This book also includes practical worksheets, such as a personal clothing inventory and a wish/want/need list, to help you organize your wardrobe and make informed shopping decisions. It emphasizes self-confidence, individuality, and smart choices in fashion and personal care.

CONTENTS

OTHER BOOKS FOR TEENS AND YOUNG ADULTS
BY THE AUTHOR iii

ABOUT THIS BOOK vii

1. WHAT YOUR APPEARANCE TELLS OTHERS
   ABOUT YOU. 1
   - What Does Your Style Say About You?
   - What Would You Like Your Clothes to Say About You?
   - The Secret to Creating a Style of Your Very Own

2. DO YOU HAVE "NOTHING TO WEAR"? 9
   - Do You REALLY Have "Nothing to Wear"?
   - Your Personal Clothing Inventory to Know What's in Your Closet and What Goes with What
   - How to Create a Shopping "Wish/Want/Need List"

3. WHAT STYLES LOOK BEST ON YOUR BODY? 29
   - How to Know What Clothes Look Good on You
   - How to Play Up Your Best Features—and Minimize Others
   - Select Cloths That Look Best on Your Body Type

4. WHAT COLORS LOOK BEST ON YOU? 39
   - Feeling "Blue"? "Green" with Envy? In the "Pink"?: The Power of Colors
   - Why Wearing the Right Color Can Make You Feel Prettier
   - Are You a "Spring", "Summer", "Winter", or "Autumn" Girl?—the "System of Seasons" and How to Determine Yours
   - Shop With Your Colors in Mind

5. **JAZZING UP YOUR LOOK WITH ACCESSORIES 51**
   - Accessories Advertise Your Style
   - Earrings, Bracelets, Necklaces, Scarves, Belts, Pins, Caps and Other Accessories: Taking Inventory
   - Using Accessories to Complement, Not Detract

6. **SHOPPING, SHOPPING, SHOPPING, SHOPPING, SHOPPING. 59**
   - Be a Smart Shopper: How to Decide What's a Wise Buy and What's Not
   - Create 30 Different Looks with 10 Articles of Clothing
   - Your Personal Shopping List to Take with You When You Shop

7. **"SCENTS-IBLE" ADVICE: WHAT YOU SHOULD KNOW ABOUT PERFUMES 71**
   - The Earlier the Hour, the Lighter the Scent: Rules for What, When and How Much to Wear
   - Pulse Points: Where to Wear Your Perfume
   - Why You Can't Smell Your Own Perfume
   - Floral, Citrus or Chypres? Choosing the Right Scent for You

CHAPTER 1

What Your Appearance Tells Others about You

There is no beauty that hath not some strangeness in its proportion.

—FRANCIS BACON

"Don't judge a book by its cover" is an honorable virtue most of us aspire to, but oftentimes we still end up forming a first impression based upon how someone looks. I remember the first time I met Brad. He was smartly dressed in clean, pressed khaki pants, a mod shirt, cool sandals, with trendy sunglasses smartly perched on top his well-groomed head of hair. Bright eyes, a friendly smile, and gleaming teeth completed the look.

One glance and I decided that this was a contemporary guy, one who knew what looked good on him and cared enough about himself to take the time to look good. Correct or not, his appearance gave off an air of "cool" and made me think:

- "This guy's in tune with his appearance. He's current."
- "This guy's immaculately groomed. I'll bet he keeps his car clean."
- "This guy's outgoing. I'll bet he's got cool and really nice friends."
- "I bet he is sensitive and kind—and a good kisser!"

Does someone's appearance influence how you think about him or her? I have to admit, that was the case for me with Brad. A person's appearance can't tell you "who" that person is, nor should it ever be a basis for judging a person's character, but it makes an impression, nonetheless. If, as they say, a picture is worth a thousand words, then my school was a colossal picture-book dictionary.

Cheryl

Cheryl always wore her skirts and tank tops very tight and very revealing. My friends thought the way she dressed wasn't appropriate for school, as well as thinking it would be uncomfortable having to spend an entire day in those things. Her appearance made us feel uncomfortable—in more ways than one. Because of the way she dressed, many girls—while polite to her—often excluded her when they wanted to just hang out on the weekends.

Megan

Megan had a "reputation" for the way she dressed, too. Megan was an artsy and whimsical girl with an outgoing personality who dressed mostly in bold prints and vibrant colors. Everyone felt that one day Megan would be somebody special in the art world. She looked the part. One of her outfits that was a favorite of mine was an ankle-length flowing skirt with contrasting geometric shapes in various shades of blue, purple, and rose, worn with a softly shaped, very long ivory sweater. To this she added an eye-catching choker of painted wooden blocks with a matching oversized bracelet.

I don't know where she shopped, but Megan had a knack for finding the most unusual shoes and artsy-craftsy jewelry. It was easy to tell from her appearance that Megan was creative and artistic; she used herself as a canvas, creating a picture that displayed her talent.

Sara

Sara was a shy and demure girl, her clothes reflecting a gentle and soft-spoken personality. In her yearbook she listed her ambition as wanting to teach elementary school. I thought she would make a good teacher for small children, especially with her reverent way of being such an attentive listener—an eye for detail that also showed up in the way she dressed. She preferred soft fabrics and small floral prints and wore mostly one-piece dresses and blouses and slacks—never Jeans and her jewelry was always dainty, very lovely. She always looked so classy, so lady-like, and elegant.

Marriah

Marriah, an outgoing and flamboyant girl, just like her wardrobe, loved bright colors and nappy fabrics. Always dramatic, Marriah wore interesting clothes and bold jewelry that matched her confidence. She told everyone she wanted "her own company." None of us doubted that one day she would have a business of her own, even if no one (including Marriah) knew just what the nature of her company might be! None of us doubted she'd be a success!

Jennifer

Comfort was my thing. In my school, team players wore jerseys on the day of a game. Basically, this was the school's display of spirit and an alert to other students that today a certain team was playing, and they should head for the bleachers and support their friends. I played three sports each year, so I was often in a uniform. When I wasn't, I still dressed in casual clothes because when I went to practice, which was usually every day after school, I knew that the clothes I wore to school that day were going to end up at the bottom of my sports bag, and I probably would not unpack them until much later that evening—or, quite possibly, until a day or two later! So, I picked my clothes for comfort, wear, and easy wash.

I'm quite sure no one ever thought of me as glamorous (well, maybe Ben!) but rather, a good athlete. Or at least I think that's what they thought. I was chosen "Most Inspirational Player" for three years in a row, even though some other students deserved it too, and even when I didn't think I'd get chosen since I had won the award the year before. Thinking back, I was seen as an athlete partly because of the casual and sporty way I dressed.

WHAT DOES YOUR APPEARANCE SAY ABOUT YOU?

No doubt about it, the clothes we wear—and the way we wear them—create an impression, one that others can readily see.

What does your appearance say about you? Are you shy or outspoken, gregarious, or laid-back? Are you sporty, artsy, or formal? In the spaces provided, jot down several words you think best describe what your appearance reveals about you.

My appearance tells others that I am a person who:

_____

_____

Ask two good friends to describe what they think your appearance says about you, and write it down in the space here. The goal is to see how their views compare to yours.

♥ _____

_____

♥ _____

_____

Here is a very important question, too: What do you WANT your appearance to tell others about you and, is your appearance giving off the message you would like it to?

_____

_____

SENDING YOUR MESSAGE WITH "STYLE"

Also evident in your appearance is your sense of style. Style is more than dressing in the latest fad or fashion or wearing colorful fabrics or intricately tailored designs. Style is about a sense of self and becomes a classic way you have of presenting yourself to the world.

The late Audrey Hepburn, a style legend, reigned as a movie star of the 1950s and 1960s. In addition to being an accomplished actress, one of Ms. Hepburn's greatest starring roles (even today!) is that of the public's ideal of someone with a supreme sense of style. As a result, her name is practically synonymous with glamour. She is considered one of the great beauties of all time. Yet she wasn't beautiful in the classic way we think of beauty. It's just that she possessed a sense of fashion that was elegance personified. Style, you see, is not about being beautiful as much as projecting an organized and balanced personal style.

DARA MONTGOMERY—OUR VERY OWN AUDREY HEPBURN

Dara Montgomery was my school's Audrey Hepburn. Dara could pull together a fabulous outfit like no one else I knew. She just had a natural talent for choosing what went with what. Be it the day of school pictures, the day our school attended a lecture at a local museum, or a sporting event or the prom, Dara showed up smartly dressed for the occasion, and she always wore an outfit that complemented the activity at hand.

It wasn't just Dara's knowing what to wear and when that made her stand out and seem so much more "with it" than the rest of us. She didn't spend a lot of money on her clothes, nor did she necessarily have a lot of clothes. Dara had a keen fashion sense about what looked good on her and why. What she did have, was a knack for combining certain pieces with others in a way that really worked, and an eye for mixing and matching certain colors that complemented her coloring and features.

I distinctly recall watching Dara walk up to the front of the class one day to hand in a paper, looking as though she could have been a fashion consultant in a nice department store. She was wearing a deep sea-green sweater with a pleated plaid skirt that swayed loosely as she moved. Draped around her shoulders was a rather large, bold, rust-colored scarf knotted in a really unique way. As always, she smelled of a fragrance as clean and simple as the understated jewelry she wore. Just a hint of eye shadow and a subdued shade of lip gloss finished off "her look," one that made Dara appear polished, poised, and complete—as usual.

Dara's look of being "polished, poised and complete" was her style, always evident in whatever she was wearing. Clearly, Dara knew something about clothes, colors, and accessorizing the rest of us didn't.

We can all learn Dara's secrets of style.

THE SECRET TO CREATING A STYLE OF YOUR OWN

Looking through fashion magazines is one good way to develop an awareness of style. Observing others around you is an even better method, since the people we see in our everyday lives are more likely to be those with whom we wish to fit in. Tune in to what others are wearing and how a certain style or color makes them look. See if you can determine what it is about another's appearance that you like—or don't like—and why.

Ask yourself:

- ⊙ **Does the person's appearance project an overall look that is attractive?** If so, give your reasons. For example, you might think, "She looks neat and well-groomed." "She looks together." "She looks comfortable."

- ⊙ **Does the particular style the person is wearing look good on her?** Again, give your reasons. For example, "That skirt length flatters her height and figure."

- ⊙ **Does the color of the outfit flatter her?** If so, why? If not, what color do you think would? For example, "That deep-purple suit is a great color for her, much better than a lighter lavender, which would seem washed out next to her dark hair, eyes and complexion." Or, "The pastel sweater looks very nice with her complexion and color of her hair."

- ⊙ **Do the accessories she is wearing look good with her outfit; do they complement the garments she is wearing?** If so, why? If not, what do you think would look better? For example, "I think that slacks would better with a belt and tie her outfit together."

AWARENESS CAN SHARPEN YOUR FASHION SENSE

An awareness of how certain styles, colors, and accessories complement the appearances of others can sharpen your own fashion sense. That's why when you're studying what does or doesn't look good on others, it's important to do more than say, "Wow, she looks great," or "That really looks awful on her." Try to figure out why something either does or doesn't work. This is information you can use to determine how certain styles, fabrics and colors might look on you.

Choosing styles that work well with your body shape and wearing colors that are most flattering to your hair and skin tone not only shows you have a fashion sense about you, but they make you look your best.

The next few chapters will show YOU how.

CHAPTER 2

Do You Have "Nothing to Wear"?

Beauty is all very well at first sight. But whoever looks at it when it has been in the house for three days?

—SAPPHO

SINGING THE "NOTHING-TO-WEAR" BLUES

How many times do you need to look your best? There's the group photo for band on Wednesday, a job interview at your favorite store on Thursday after school, and you're hoping a special someone will take notice when you casually ask whether or not he's got a date for the upcoming dance. Almost every day, you have a reason to look your personal best. And as often, you rummage through your closet searching for the perfect outfit to wear, but nothing feels right. You try on dress after pants after skirt, posing in front of the mirror and sighing, "I have nothing to wear!" —only to be reminded by your mother, "You have a closet full of clothes!"

You know she's right. So how is it that you can't find anything that looks or feels right?

WHY DON'T YOU HAVE ANYTHING TO WEAR?

If you identify with the nothing-to-wear blues, you aren't alone. But let's see if you can determine why you have nothing to wear.

Do you have "nothing to wear" because:

- ☹ You look like a tent in the red sweater you bought last month;
- ☹ The new style of pants that made your best friend look really cool makes you look positively awful;
- ☹ You loaned out your favorite skirt and your friend has not re-turned it;
- ☹ The bright-yellow blouse you thought you'd love doesn't go with anything in your closet;
- ☹ Your extra-wide belt is so out-of-date;
- ☹ You don't have a single pair of shoes that looks good with your new dress.

If these and other reasons are true for you, then of course you have nothing to wear when in reality, you:

- ☹ Forget about some of the things you have;
- ☹ Don't like the way certain things fit you;
- ☹ Are tired of wearing that one "standby" outfit that is so comfortable and looks so nice on you that you reach for it time and again;
- ☹ Forget to launder garments when needed so an item is not clean on the day you want to wear it;
- ☹ Don't like the color of a certain item;
- ☹ Don't want to wear the garments that are now "out of style";
- ☹ Can't keep track of what you've loaned out and to whom;
- ☺ Would like to buy something new.

YOUR CLOSET: HOME FOR THE PERFECT WARDROBE

A good way to get a handle on the nothing-to-wear blues is to take inventory. The goal is to think about all the clothes, belts, and shoes you already own—your wardrobe. Identify all the clothes and shoes in your closet, and your dresser drawers, your clothes hamper, in the trunk of the car, the laundry room as well as those that may be hanging in your friend's closet.

Don't forget the loose shoe or articles of clothing that may have tried to run away and are now hiding under your bed! And don't forget those items you've been meaning to retrieve from the "Lost and Found" bin at school, as well as any other place you could have left certain items. By assessing your wardrobe, you will know what you own but don't wear—and why—and can better determine what you need in order to wear other pieces.

At the end of this chapter, you will find a Personal Clothing Inventory worksheet. The inventory is designed to help you itemize all the clothing, belts, shoes, and accessories you have. This Inventory will help you get a very clear picture of your wardrobe so you'll get a better idea why you don't like or don't wear certain pieces—all of which can be a big reason you "don't have anything to wear." The Inventory can be helpful because it:

- ✔ Is a good visual, a way to see all the items you have;
- ✔ Helps to clarify why you may not be wearing certain pieces but would if only you had the right pair of pants, the right kind and color of shoes, and so on;
- ✔ Helps you remember items that you've forgotten all about, and to get new ideas for coordinating different articles of clothing;
- ✔ Helps determine what items to give away or "trade" with a friend who likes a certain item and gives you an item in return;
- ✔ Helps you identify what you need so that you can ask for it as a birthday gift or look for it the next time you go shopping.

SASHA LINN'S INVENTORY

The Inventory of Sasha Linn appears on the following pages. Glance through it so that you will have an idea how yours will look after you've completed it.

As you are looking over Sasha's inventory, notice the four columns: Item, Fabric, Color, and Comments. Also notice the general headings under items: pants, skirts, dresses, blouses, sweaters, jackets, Ts, jumpers, shoes, belts, and accessories.

Itemizing your things according to kind is a good way to see exactly what you have and can pinpoint reasons why you may or may not be wearing certain things. For example, let's say you're getting ready for school and decide you'll wear that great new top you bought over the weekend. So, you pull on the new top and then search for a pair of slacks to wear with it but feel nothing looks quite right. "I have no pants!" you declare. But in fact, you have four pairs, just none look great with your new top!

If you knew exactly what you owned prior to shopping, you would have known that you should have also shopped for a pair of slacks or a skirt to wear with your new top—or purchased some other top that would go with what you already owned.

I'll explain the Fabric, Color, and Comments columns later in this chapter. Right now, look over Sasha's Inventory to get a feel for how it works.

ITEM	FABRIC	COLOR	COMMENTS

PANTS

ITEM	FABRIC	COLOR	COMMENTS
Capri	Cotton / Spandex	Beige	Very comfortable
Overalls	Cotton	Blue	Very comfortable, but needs hemming
Slacks	Don't Know	Black	Starting to show wear
Blue Jeans	Denim	Black	Too small, tight
Blue Jeans	Denim	Light Blue	Looks great with Ts
Blue Jeans	Denim	Faded Blue	Live in these; great fit
Pants (casual)	Twill	Blue	Matching jacket

Khaki Pants	Khaki	Beige	Comfortable; looks great
Blue Jeans	Denim	Faded Blue	Holes in knees, butt area. Can wear only sometimes
Blue Jeans	Denim	Red	Don't like
Blue Jeans	Denim	Dark Blue	Don't like style

SKIRTS

Straight flowered	Cotton	Multi	Casual—looks good with T-shirts
Ankle length	Cotton	Multi br/gold	Western look; have to be really in the mood to wear
Short skirt	Don't Know	Navy	Love it! My dance skirt
Short skirt	Denim	Flowered	Looks great with ts
Full skirt	Linen	Blue	Ruined in the wash!
Mini	Slinky	Black	Mom won't let me wear any longer; still love it
Mini	Denim	Faded Blue	Too small, outgrown

DRESSES

Casual long	Polyester	Flowers	Wear to church a lot
Knee length, Decorative buttons	Cotton Knit	Deep Blue	A great dress-up look
Formal two-piece	Wool	Hunter Green	Works with dressy blouse, too
Sundress	Cotton	Multi	Can wear in summer only

BLOUSES

Long Sleeves	Cotton	White	I live in this
Striped Long-Sleeve Shirt	Cotton	Black/White	Looks great with jeans
Short Sleeves	Cotton	Yellow	Should give away
2 Long sleeves	Cotton	White	Don't like Showing wear / Old
Blouse	Shiny	Beige	Where is it? Can't find.

SWEATERS

Long Sleeves	Knit	Ivory	Goes with everything
Bulky	Present from Aunt Sue	Purple	Makes me look like a big grape
Long Sleeves	Knit	Tan	Great with long skirt
Short Sleeves	Knit	Stripes	Don't like
Cropped cardigan	Don't Know	Black	Really like
3 Others		Assorted	Old / Boring Should Toss

JACKETS

Jacket	Twill	Blue	Matching pants
Has School Logo	Leather	Black	Couldn't live without it!
Erin Borrowed This	Denim	Blue	Must get back from Erin
Jacket	Denim	Black	Where is this?
Jacket	Denim	White	Doesn't go with anything!

Ts

Tee	Cotton	White	Own four! Live in these!
Tee	Cotton	Black	Live in this!
Tee	Cotton	White	Very washed out
Tee with University Logo	Cotton	Yellow	New / Love it My Favorite Team!
Tee with School Logo	Cotton	Navy	Wear to school games

JUMPERS

Knee length	Don't know	Beige	Boring, never did like this
Ankle length	Nylon	Dark Brown	Boring, but wear a lot
Mini	Denim	Faded Blue	Wear on library days
V-Neck	Linen	Sand	Always looks wrinkled

SHOES

Nine West Platforms	Leather	Brown	Love 'em
Tennis	Canvas	White	Love 'em
Nike Swoops	Canvas	White/Black	Wear a lot
Loafers	Leather	Brown	Wear a lot
Casual slip-ons	Upper is cloth	Beige	Wear with skirts
3-inch Heels	Leather	Navy	Not very comfortable
Loafers	Leather	Navy	Not very comfortable
Heels	Leather	Floral	Don't go with anything
Kitten Heels	Cloth	Pink	From my sister's wedding / Should dye black for prom dress?

BELTS

Belt	Western	Black	Wear it all the time
Belt	Leather stitch	Black	Wear a lot
Belt	Cloth	Black	Worn out; holes stretched
Belt	Leather	Black	Too small
Belt	Plastic	White	Ugly; never wear
Belt	Patent Leather	Black	Wear a lot
Belt	Woven Leather	Navy	Falling apart
Belt	Leather	Red	Too small
Belt	Leather	White	Too short for low-waisted pants and skirts

RINGS

Class ring		Gold	Never take off
Assorted (10)	Have had for years	Silver	Junky, almost never wear
Ring	Flower	Plastic	Fun / Love it

NECKLACES

Faux Pearls			Mostly wear to church (also wore to prom)
Assorted (5)		3 Silver 2 Gold (1 broken)	I really don't like to wear necklaces

EARRINGS

Faux pearls			Matches necklace
Loops (3 pairs)		2 Gold 1 Silver	Live in these Lost one
Others (8 pairs)		Old junk	Out of style; tarnished; broken

BRACELETS

Bracelets			Wear sometimes
Bracelets		3 Gold 2 Silver 1 Green String 2 Mixed Beads	I actually don't like to wear bracelets because they break in gym class and playing sports

PURSES

Purse	Floral Print	Spring	Can use only in spring and summer
Purse		Silver, Glittery	Prom
Purse		Black	Handle broken, should toss
Purse		Brown	Old (but use daily) Tattered

SCARVES, CAPS, HATS

Cap	Dallas Cowboys	Royal Blue	Love it
Hat	Straw		Old but still use
Cap		Red	School Team Spirit
Caps		Blue/White	Old Never Wear

HOW TO INVENTORY YOUR WARDROBE

Okay, so that's the idea. As you can see from looking over Sasha's Inventory, it's a pretty straight forward task. Now it's your turn.

You'll find your copy of Your Personal Clothing Inventory on the next page. Since you'll be needing it as you go through the next several chapters, complete it as soon as you can. It's going to take you a good hour or so, so you may want to schedule doing it at a time when you can put on your favorite music and plow in.

It would also be a fun activity to do with your best friend.

Here's a suggestion: You may want to make a copy of this worksheet before you complete it so that you'll have an extra copy to use when you'd like to take stock of your things again. You may even want to give a copy of it to a friend, so she can inventory her things, as well. (You can also create your own inventory just by using lined notebook paper.)

Here are the steps:

Step 1: Under the column PANTS, list your favorite pair.

Step 2: The next column is FABRIC. Jot down the material or fabric.

Step 3: The next column is COLOR. Write down the color of this pair of pants.

Step 4: The next column is COMMENTS. Here add a comment as to what you like or dislike about the item of clothing, such as "love it" or "makes me look and feel great!" or "needs hemming," or "loaned to a friend," or "need to get back," and so on. Be as thorough as you can.

Step 5: Now list your next-favorite pair of pants, or the ones you wear the most, and then list the fabric, color, and comment. Do this for each pair of pants you have, beginning with the ones you wear and like the most, working your way down to listing those you wear the least—or not at all.

Step 6: Do this for each and every item in your closet.

Step 7: Inventory your shoes, belts, jewelry, and other accessories, including handbags if you own more than a couple.

YOUR PERSONAL CLOTHING INVENTORY

Name:

ITEM	FABRIC	COLOR	COMMENTS

PANTS

SKIRTS

DRESSES

BLOUSES

SWEATERS

JACKETS

Ts

JUMPERS

SHOES

BELTS

RINGS

NECKLACES

EARRINGS

PURSES

BRACELETS

ADDITIONAL ITEMS (SUCH AS SCARVES, CAPS, HATS)

ANY SURPRISES?

Once the inventory is completed, review it carefully.

Are you surprised by the length of your itemized list? Do you have a lot of clothes, or not as many as you thought?

_____

_____

Do you notice anything *telling*? For example, do you have several favorite garments, such as skirts, that you don't presently wear because you don't have the right kinds of shoes to wear with them?

_____

_____

Are there three or more items on the list you noted as "out of style" or "doesn't fit"?

_____

_____

In the next few chapters, I'll address some of the most common "closet quandaries" such as, "I don't like the way it looks on me," or "the color is all wrong!" and help you discover why that is, and what you can do to dress with style and pizzazz to look your personal best!

Don't forget to keep your Clothing Inventory handy! You'll need it as you read throughout the rest of the chapters.

CHAPTER 3

What Styles Look Best on Your Body?

The perception of beauty is a moral test.

—HENRY DAVID THOREAU

DO YOUR CLOTHES LOOK GOOD ON YOU?

In reviewing the Comments column of your CLOTHING INVENTORY, did you find that one of the reasons you don't wear a certain item is because "I don't like the way it looks on me"? For most of us, that's the number one complaint as to why an article of clothing doesn't get worn often.

If a certain article of clothing doesn't look quite right on you, why is that? Is it because you have outgrown it, or that you don't like the color? Is it because it reminds you of a time with a certain friend who is no longer your friend? Or is it that the outfit simply isn't designed for your body type?

Maybe it doesn't look quite right on you because it's not really right for you.

Every girl can wear skirts, pants, and dresses. We just can't all wear the *same* skirts, pants, and dresses. How we look in something is often determined by our shape, and more precisely, our bodyline.

Girls are often overly critical about their shape. It's one of the most common complaints I hear. Girls often say to each other, "I wish I had your figure!" or "I wish I were as tall as you!"

"Perfect" stereotypes feed off our insecurities and only serve to make us unhappy with our own natural beauty. Besides, our ideal of "perfect" constantly changes. The "It Girl" of the 1950s was Marilyn Monroe, petite and voluptuous. In today's time, Ms. Monroe would probably be considered slightly overweight.

In the 1960s a model called "Twiggy" set the standard, and many girls said they wished they could be as tall and thin as she was. In today's time, we would probably consider Twiggy to have a weight problem, too—like, being too thin!

The mid- to late-1980s brought us Madonna—five feet, five inches, fit, toned, savvy and sassy—while the early 1990s ushered in Cindy Crawford, followed by the minimalist look, followed by the wholesome and healthy looks. Luckily, we now have a healthier idea of the importance of accepting ourselves for what we are—and make the most of it.

The goal is to be healthy and fit—and to not compare yourself to others but rather, to understand your body shape and dress to look your personal best.

HOW TO BE YOUR OWN "IT GIRL"

Even if your school's "It Girls" are very different from you, instead of trying to become them, work with what you have. By studying your features and bodylines, you can learn how to dress in a way that compliments or plays up your best features, while downplaying or detracting attention from those things you don't like as much. Again, a reminder: your body is still growing and changing. Enjoy the styles you can wear now. And be ready to leave them behind when it's time to move on.

Understanding your "bodyline" is a first step in selecting clothing that is most flattering to you. A remark such as "I'm tall" or "I'm short" may be a good way of describing your height, but it's only one part of the picture when it comes to describing your body shape. If you were to add, "I'm small-boned" or "I'm large-boned," that would be another piece, but it still isn't enough. Nor is mentioning how much you weigh.

A more important consideration is the shape of your body. The question, "Are you more straight or rounded?" offers more useful information in determining what styles look best on you.

STRAIGHT BODY SHAPE VS. CURVED BODY SHAPE

Karen is seven inches taller than Rianna. Do you think they both look good in the same style? Probably not.

Rianna's bodyline would fall into the "round" category. Rianna has a rounded shape, whereas Karen has straight lines. Neither girl can change her bone structure, but they can dress in those styles that help them achieve the look each of them wants.

Which of the two body types do you think best describes you?

My bodyline is:
- ☐ More straight than curvy;
- ☐ More curvy than straight.

HOW TO DETERMINE WHAT LOOKS GOOD ON YOUR BODY

We often think we know the shape of our bodies. But when you try this next exercise, you'll see how different even our own perception of our body can be from what we think it is.

A good way to determine your shape or "bodyline," as professional tailors call it, is to trace the outline of your body. The result is a visual that can reveal a great deal of information, one you can use in thinking about the styles that look best on your frame.

Tape a large sheet of paper to a wall—the kind that's used to cover tables—and then ask your mom or a good friend to use a marker pen to trace around your body. Stand with your back to the wall. Trace from head to toe, then stand back and look at the outline of the figure you see.

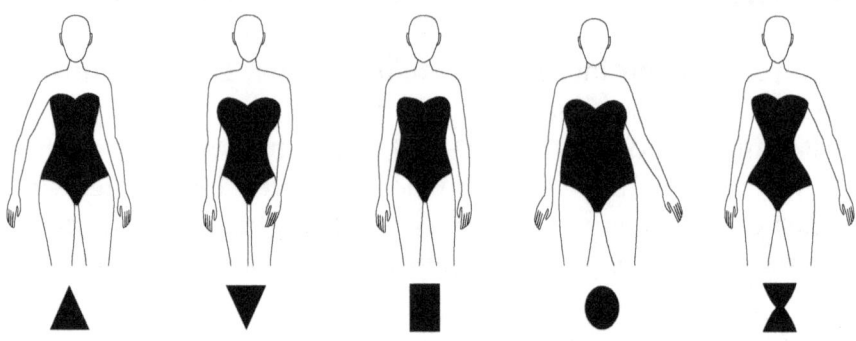

You may be surprised at what you find. When my friend Jessica did this, she was surprised to discover an outline that revealed a "straight body" without much of a waistline or hips. *"I honestly thought of myself differently than what the picture revealed,"* Jessica remarked. *"I was always trying to gain weight so that I could have hips. But I can see from the outline that I do have hips, it's just that I have virtually no waistline. My body is a perfect balance of 'straight.' I've decided to declare a truce with my body and rid myself of the negative feeling of not liking my shape. I'm better off learning how to choose clothes that flatter my bone structure and bodylines. By wearing the styles that flatter me, I can still achieve the look I want."*

Jessica has discovered the key to looking more stylish: Your bodyline is an important consideration in selecting clothes that look good on your body type.

DRESS TO COMPLEMENT YOUR SHAPE

Regardless of your shape, whether you have straight lines and wish you had a curved shape, or have a curved shape and wish you it wasn't quite as curvy, by learning how to select clothes that complement your shape, you can look sharp and stylish.

It's not possible to go into all the variations on how to select the clothes that are ideal for your body type in this chapter. My intent is to help you understand the principle behind dressing with your bodylines in mind.

Here's what fashion experts have to say:

If your bodyline is more straight than curvy, then:
- ▸ Straight styles in plain colors or linear prints (stripes and plaids) will look best on you.
- ▸ Accessories and jewelry in rectangular or geometric shapes look good on you.

If you are large-boned or on the heavy side, then:
- ▸ Larger patterns and accessories work well on you;
- ▸ Vertical lines look good on you.

If your bodyline is more curvy than straight, then:
- ▸ A jacket with a fitted waist brings out the beauty of your natural shapeliness.
- ▸ Plain colors and prints are more flattering to you than stripes or plaids.
- ▸ Accessories in rounded earrings and necklace shapes suit you best.

If you are small-boned and petite, then:
- ▸ You can wear small prints or thin stripes well.
- ▸ You look better in smaller earrings and thin chained necklaces.
- ▸ Wide stripes or huge prints and big earrings that are flattering to a larger person will completely overpower you.

Take note that some clothing shapes, such as those with a softened line that are neither too straight nor too curved, work well for both curved and straight body types. Try it and you will see that you and your mirror agree.

Again, this is only the tip of the information available to help you dress your personal best. Most major department stores employ fashion consultants and personal shoppers. This is a good source of advice, as well. And don't forget your life skills courses at school. Information pertinent to understanding the principles of style was offered in my school. Check to see if it is offered at yours, or look for information on-line and of course, ask your mom, too.

HOW TO PLAY UP YOUR BEST FEATURES— AND MINIMIZE AREAS YOU DON'T "LIKE"

The good news is that you can almost always maximize the effect of your best features and minimize the ones you don't like. Below are just a few of the ways to play up your best features and camouflage others—to make your "flaws" work to your advantage and look your personal best.

NECK

- **Problem:** My neck is too long.
- **Solution:** Wear turtlenecks, scarves, or chokers to shorten its appearance.

- **Problem:** My neck is too short.
- **Solution:** A scoop, V-neckline or an open collar will make it appear longer. Vertical features, such as long necklaces, scarves and bows tied low, or ruffles down the front of your blouse, will also give the image of a longer neck.

SHOULDERS

- **Problem:** My shoulders are too narrow.

- **Solution:** Shoulder pads were invented for you. If your facial features are rounded, you'll look better in smaller, softer shoulder pads. If your face is more angular, use larger square or epaulet shoulder pads. Another way to broaden your shoulders is to choose garments with shoulder seams slightly outside your shoulder bones. The same goes for sleeveless dresses: The fabric should end outside your shoulder bones. A cap sleeve also broadens the shoulder.

- **Problem:** My shoulders are too broad.

- **Solution:** Stay away from shoulder pads, boat necklines (they draw the eye across, emphasizing the shoulder line) and details at the shoulder. You'll look great in a V- or scoop-neck with a soft shoulder look, or raglan (loosely fitted) sleeves. Non-fitted sleeve styles (raglan, batwing, kimono) pull the eye inward and down, so they look best on persons with broad or square shoulders.

ARMS

- **Problem:** My arms are too big.

- **Solution:** Avoid sleeves that are tight or clingy.

- **Problem:** My arms are too short.

- **Solution:** A three-quarter sleeve makes the arm, and the entire torso, appear longer. Cuffs shorten the arm, so avoid cuffs.

- **Problem:** My arms are too long.

- **Solution:** Cuffs shorten the appearance of the arm. A girl with long arms may have trouble finding long sleeves that reach her wrist, but this doesn't have to keep you from buying that outfit you love if you consider adding a cuff to it.

BUST

- **Problem:** My bust is too large.

- **Solution:** A short sleeve draws the eye up; if you're large busted, go for short sleeves that end above or below the bustline (rather than right at the bustline). You can also draw attention from your bustline by wearing darker colors on top. Open necklines, long sleeves and loose-fitting clothes with vertical stripes or piping on the bodice will minimize your bustline, too. Avoid tight-fitting tops, chest pockets and high waistbands. Avoid low necklines and high waistlines, which will attract attention to your bustline.

- **Problem:** My bust is too small.

- **Solution:** If you have a small bustline and you'd like it to appear larger, try wearing textured materials and tweeds, loose-fitting tops with high necklines (turtlenecks and cowl necklines are great), yokes, or bodices with details like pockets, bows, ties, buttons, gathers, pleats or embroidery. You can also enhance your bustline by wearing a bra with padding.

WAISTLINE

- **Problem:** I'm too short-waisted.

- **Solution:** A skirt with a yoke around the hips, a dropped waist, or no waistband at all will help to lengthen your upper body. A medium-to-narrow belt the same color as your top will have the same effect.

- **Problem:** My upper torso is too long.

- **Solution:** An empire waist (high, just under the bustline) or a wide belt the same color and fabric as your skirt will help to shorten a long torso.

HIPS

- **Problem:** My hips are too large.

- **Solution:** A long over-blouse with a dropped belt draws attention away from your hips, so they will appear smaller. Gathered skirts, loose pleats, hip pockets, and decorative details at the hipline accentuate your hips, so stick with stitched-down or inverted pleats. Wear pants and skirts in deep solid colors. Avoid patterns and light colors on the bottom.

- **Problem:** My hips are too flat.

- **Solution:** If you want to make your hips appear to be more filled out, go for those styles that have pockets and hipline decoration. Gathered skirts and loose pleats also work for you.

LEGS

- **Problem:** My legs are very long and gangly looking.

- **Solution:** Wear skirts with a yoke, hemlines at or below the knee, or long pants with pleats and cuffs.

- **Problem:** My legs are too short.

- **Solution:** A short skirt will make your legs appear longer. You can also achieve this effect with a high waistline, cropped pant legs and stockings that match your shoes or skirt.

FEET

- **Problem:** My feet are too big.

- **Solution:** Wear shoes that fit the shape of your foot without adding the appearance of additional length or width. Boots and platform shoes will make your feet look bigger, as will decorations such as buckles, bows and tassels. Darker colors will make your feet appear smaller; whites and pastels always make feet appear larger.

- **Problem:** My feet are too small.

- **Solution:** Wear shoes that fit yet add the illusion of size such as wide heels and thick soles. You can also achieve a larger look with multi-colored shoes as well as those with fancy decor such as straps, tassels, buckles and bows.

Knowing your body and understanding what looks good on you is an important first step in looking your personal best.

While I've been discussing bodyline and dressing in a way that enhances your appearance, remember that being healthy and fit is always a priority.

Aside from wearing clothes that enhance your appearance, what else can you do to look and feel your best?

_____

_____

In the following chapter, you'll see what a big effect color can have on you and your appearance.

CHAPTER 4

What Colors Look Best on YOU?

Vow to be valiant; resolve to be radiant; determine to be dynamic; strive to be sincere; aspire to be attuned.

—WILLIAM ARTHUR WARD

You probably know that some colors on you look better than others. Wearing the "right" colors for you can really make a difference. You might be surprised at just how much. Think about the last time you wore a color you really like. Did it:

- ✔ Make someone remark, "You look great in that color"?
- ✔ Bring out your natural beauty?
- ✔ Get you noticed; did others look at you and you noticed?
- ✔ Reduce your stress levels?
- ✔ Make you more self-confident?
- ✔ Make you feel happier?

Wearing the "right" color can make the difference in how you look—and feel!

FEELING "BLUE"? "GREEN" WITH ENVY? IN THE "PINK": THE POWER OF COLORS

When you forget to study for a test and it's upsetting because you got a bad grade and you're bummed about it, do you say, "I'm feeling blue"?

When you are upset because the special someone you like asked someone else to the dance, do you say, "I'm almost green with envy"?

Ever hear a cowboy in a Western movie talk about a coward and say, "He's yellow"?

When you visit your grandmother does she say, "Now that you're here, I'm feeling in the pink today"?

If you think about it, you'll realize that you talk about colors all the time. Color is often the first quality you use to describe something. For example, you don't say, "I bought a cotton shirt" but rather, "I bought a blue cotton shirt." When you describe a friend, you're likely to say, "She has brown hair and brown eyes."

Because color has so much power over your life, it's important that you know how to use color to your advantage. Psychologists have done studies proving that colors can do things like cheer people up (red seems to make people happy), calm people down (pink is soothing). Hospitals often paint rooms green because it is a "healing" color, and blue appears to help people stay focused on a task, to concentrate harder.

WHAT IS YOUR FAVORITE COLOR?

What is your favorite color and why?

_____

Do you have a lot of clothes in that color? Do you buy things like backpacks and book covers in that color? My friend loves pink. She painted her bedroom pink. She has pink sheets and blankets. She has a pink slipcover over the seat of her car. And the car has a bumper sticker that reads THINK PINK! We tease her about all this, but Keesha just shrugs and says, "Pink makes me happy."

HOW COLORS CAN MAKE YOU LOOK AND FEEL PRETTIER

Colors can do more than make your feel good; they can make you look good. You already know that certain colors complement your face, while other colors make you look washed-out or sallow. When you wear your bright turquoise silk shirt, do people tell you that you're looking especially pretty that day? I have an aquamarine sweater that is very bright and cheerful. Whenever I wear it, my girlfriends tell me that I'm "looking happy." It's just that the sweater is really my color and makes me feel good.

Why is that? To know which colors look best on you, you need to understand a little bit about colors themselves. I was looking for a new dress to wear to a very special party. I was a senior in high school at the time. The salesclerk asked me what I had in mind, and I said, "I'd like something in a really pretty color. I know all my friends will be in colorful dresses, but I feel better in earth-tone colors." The clerk smiled and said, "Oh, you must be an 'Autumn Girl.'"

Autumn girl? I had never heard that term before. I asked the clerk what she meant, and she and I got into a really interesting discussion about "having your colors done." Have you ever heard that expression?

THE "SYSTEM OF SEASONS"

The "System of Seasons" is about the shades each of us look best in based upon our hair and eye coloring and the tone of our skin. For example, a "Spring girl" is usually blonde or has sandy brown hair with very light skin. She probably has blue or hazel eyes. This coloring makes her look nice in colors like apricot, coral, red, yellow, and aqua. My good friend Sarah is a Spring, as is my mother.

My friends Randee and Nghin are "Autumn" girls, like me. Autumn girls have gray-green or brown eyes, chestnut hair, or red hair (from auburn to coppery red to "carrot top"), and skin with a yellowish tinge. Autumn girls look great in earth tones, like brown, gold, and beiges, but not so great in deep blues. When Sarah dyed her hair black and began wearing a much darker makeup, she looked completely different when wearing colors like apricot or yellow. Normally these soft colors created a halo around her and when she dyed her hair black, the colors created an almost stark appearance.

Of course, you can wear whatever color you like. And you should. The advantage of knowing your "season" is that you can complement the color of your hair, eyes, and skin tone—this is a real bonus in looking your very best, even in feeling your very best.

Right now, if you were to guess what "season" you are, what would you chose, and why?

_____

_____

Do you know anyone who knows what color of "Season" she is and if so, what does she day about it?

_____

_____

Have you ever had your "colors done" or would like to?

_____

_____

This next section can help you learn more about how to identify your "season."

WHAT "SEASON ARE YOU?

Below is a chart to help you identify your season, as well as highlight those colors that look best on you.

Season	Hair	Eyes	Skin	Best Colors
SPRING	Light	Light	Fair	Clear, Warm, Crisp Colors: Pink, Apricot, Salmon, Coral, Gold
SUMMER	Light	Light	Rosy	Pastels, Neutrals, Rose, Most Blues, Lavender
AUTUMN	Reddish	Hazel	Golden	Muted or Clear Earth Tones; Teal, Periwinkle, Gold, Oyster White
WINTER	Dark	Dark	Olive and Dark	Navy Blue, Black, Pure White Clear, Cool Colors, True Red, Turquoise, Navy Blue, Black, Pure White

ARE YOU A SPRING, SUMMER, AUTUMN, OR WINTER GIRL?

There are, of course, some variations, but for the most part, these seasonal recommendations ring true. My goal is to help you understand the idea that certain colors work best for some girls but may not necessarily look vibrant and appealing on others. Use this knowledge of your hair, eyes, and skin tone to select those colors that are really special for you especially at those times when you want to "shine." You might also want to put this information to the test. Think about the girls at school who always seem so well-dressed, so put together. Can you identify which seasons they are? Do they look better in some colors than in others?

Color charts for these four seasons are everywhere; google color charts for your season to get a better idea of its usefulness.

Let's take a look at the "four seasons."

WHAT IS FRESH FOR "SPRING" GIRLS

My friend Tawny Flippen is a typical "Spring" with golden hair tones, blue eyes, and peachy skin tone. Spring girls have a wide array to choose from. If you are a Spring, you look pretty in apricot, salmon, coral, and pink—but rose and mauve are not so good on a Spring. Any light orange, bright coral or orange-red looks good on you.

Clear red is good but avoid a red with a bluish tint and colors that are muted. You can wear yellow, yellow-green, medium, and bright greens, many shades of aqua and turquoise, teal and peacock blue, light true blue, periwinkle blue and medium violet. Your best white is creamy ivory and you wear beige and camel well. Clear golds, rusts, and browns from golden tan to chocolate also look good on you. You can wear a light yellowish-gray, but rarely a true gray. A light, clear navy blue or black is good. Spring's colors are clear, bright, or delicate with yellow undertones.

WHAT'S HOT FOR "SUMMER" GIRLS

Renee Moreno is a typical "Summer": ash hair, gray-blue eyes, and a rosy complexion. If you are a Summer girl, you look awesome in pastels and soft neutral colors. Avoid sharp contrasts in colors, since they will leave you looking washed out. Blues were made for you, soft but ranging from light to deep, including aqua and blues with a pinkish cast, all the way to mauve and orchid, and even fuchsia, plum, burgundy arid raspberry with a powdered finish.

You look superb in soft pinks and roses, and your browns and beiges should have a rose undertone. Your navy should have a gray cast to it, keeping it soft Red, gray and green tempered with a hint of blue, are good for you. Except for a light lemon color, yellows and golds are best avoided, as are all colors with yellow undertones. You should also stay away from black, and your White should be very soft. Summer's colors are soft and cool with blue undertones. Again, color charts for these four seasons are everywhere; google color charts for your season to get a better idea how it can work for you.

THE SHADES OF "AUTUMN" GIRLS

My natural coloring is that of a typical "Autumn": warm brown hair with highlights of red or blonde, hazel eyes and olive-toned skin. If you're an Autumn girl, you have a lot of colors to choose from. You can wear either muted or clear tones. You wear all earth tones well—browns, golds, yellows, greens, oranges and orange-reds. Blues are the area where you have the least adaptability, so stick to strong and muted turquoise, and teal and deep periwinkle. You look pretty in oyster white, a white with a beige tone. You look good in all beiges except rosy beige and gray-beige. Black, navy, gray, pink and colors with blue undertones are not for you.

If you are an Autumn girl like me, our best colors are those that are stronger than Spring's and have gold or orange overtones. Again, color charts for these four seasons are everywhere; google them for your season.

WHAT'S COOL FOR "WINTER" GIRLS

Lena Arceo is a typical "Winter" girl: dark hair and eyes, beige, tan, olive, or dark skin. Winter girls look best in clear colors with sharp contrasts. The key is to keep your colors clear and vivid and to avoid anything with a yellowish cast. Your colors are strong, and solids are better for you than prints, especially near your face. You shine in icy colors (so pale you'd almost think they were white). Stay away from muted tones and powdered pastels. Clear reds and greens, blues, and turquoises, all the bluish shades of pink, and purples were made for you. You wear navy and burgundy well. You look fabulous in true white, true black and true grays from light to charcoal. Beiges are not great for you, but you can wear clear taupe (gray-beige). You can get away with a clear, bright lemon yellow, but stay away from golden yellow, gold, and golden brown.

Remember: Winter's colors are vivid, clear, or icy with blue undertones. Be sure to google the color chart for your season.

SHOP WITH YOUR COLORS IN MIND—AND IN HAND

If this is your first introduction to wearing the colors that look best on you, it can seem like a lot of trouble. But once you see and feel the difference a certain color makes, you will get better and better at selecting clothing with your best colors in mind.

Using your newfound information, go back again to Your Personal Clothing Inventory. Thinking about the colors that work best with your hair and eye coloring and your skin tone, would you say that most of the clothes in your wardrobe are in the colors that best complement you?

If you look great in bright colors but not so great in pastels, a closet full of pastels tell you that it's time to shop with your color chart in hand.

Once you have a better idea of what colors look best on you, you'll want to buy clothes in those colors. You may even want to get swatches of your colors. These are professional kits that show the colors of each season not only on paper, but in actual fabrics. You can buy these in some department stores and fabric stores, and you can order them online. If you get your "colors done" by someone who has been specifically trained (check with a salesclerk at your department stores), as a rule that person will give you a swatch of your preferred colors as a courtesy.

Short of that, go to a fabric store with two of your good friends. Hold up different fabrics close to your face and ask your friends to tell you which colors make you look your prettiest. Tell your friends to concentrate on your face, not on the fabric. A fabric store is a wonderful place to "do your colors" because of the wide variety of shades and hues of material.

Knowing which colors DON'T work for you can save you a lot of time and even more importantly—money. What if you saw an adorable little dress and just had to have it? You might buy it even without trying it on if you were in a hurry—only to get home and realize that though the cut and style are okay, but there's something about the color that just doesn't work for you. Had you known that earth colors were not good for you, you could have passed on buying it in the first place.

Just because the mannequin with black hair, dark eyes and glossy red lip color looked spectacular in that bright-red dress, if you have blue eyes and ash brown hair, it may not look as hot on you as you had hoped. Again, certain colors and certain styles look better on us than others do. It's why the mannequins come equipped with an assortment of wig colors, and their eyes and lips are often painted over to bring out the best in the fabric, color and fashion being displayed!

Another helpful suggestion is now that you have an idea of how colors and seasons work, try to get help from a salesperson who shares your season. She'll be much better at spotting the right colors for you. This is especially important if you shop with a friend of a different season coloring, as she will naturally (and unconsciously) tend to suggest colors that would look better on her.

A DOSE OF DASHING DAZZLE

I have one final comment on the power of colors. My high school's colors were red and white. Every Friday was school Spirit Day, and everyone was supposed to wear red and white. One girl in school always wore the same red and white that the rest of us did, but for some reason, while the rest of us looked like clones, she always stood apart from us and managed to look very chic.

I realized what was different. Blue was Kim's color; next to her face, it looked great. If Kim wore a red sweater, she would have a little scarf wrapped around her neck, drawing attention away from the huge red sweatshirt that made us all look like giant apples.

It was just a small dash of dazzling colors that made her always look so put-together.

SHOPPING WITH YOUR COLORS IN MIND

Now that you have identified your "Season" and specifically the Colors that look best on you, using the next pages, create a useful list you can take with you shopping.

First, go back and look back at your Clothing Inventory in Chapter 2, this time with your colors in mind.

Of the clothing you need, what colors should you select that would look best on you?

The next few pages can help.

SEASON	HAIR	EYES	SKIN	BEST COLORS

My season is:
_____

My chart identifies my best colors for this season as:

_____

_____

_____

_____

_____

The clothes in my closet that are in these colors are:

- _____
- _____
- _____
- _____
- _____
- _____
- _____
- _____
- _____
- _____

The things I've identified as needing to replace or buy as additional things I need include:

- _____
- _____
- _____
- _____
- _____
- _____
- _____
- _____

Other ways I can use my "best" colors to add beauty and pizzazz to my wardrobe:

_____

_____

_____

_____

_____

    With a little thought, you can dress to suit your body type, and your coloring, and your personality to look your personal best.

    The next chapter will show you how you can accessorize—add bracelets, earrings, scarves, and necklaces as Kim did in the example—to add pizzazz to the way you look, as well as to change the overall look of your outfit.

CHAPTER 5

Jazzing Up Your Look with Accessories

Remember the most beautiful things in the world are the most useless, peacocks and lilies, for instance.

—JOHN RUSKIN

DO YOU WEAR YOUR BOYFRIEND'S RING ON A CHAIN?

Carrie did. All through our senior year, my friend Carrie wore her boyfriend's ring on a chain around her neck.

- ♥ When she was wearing sweatshirts and other casual clothes, it hung on a long, heavy silver chain; it looked really cool.
- ♥ When she wore it with her black velour floor-length prom dress, the ring hung on a shorter silver chain that sparkled; it looked elegant.
- ♥ When she wore a formal business suit on the day of a class interview contest, she added a scarf using her boyfriend's ring as a clamp; it looked sophisticated.

Accessories are like that. One piece can dress up one outfit and then, with just a little imagination, the same piece can look fantastic in an entirely different way with a completely different outfit.

FOR BETTER OR WORSE

Accessories add, or detract, from style. Earrings, bracelets, necklaces, scarves, belts, even pins, can change the look of your outfit for better or for worse. Maybe you have a friend who always wears scarves. Scarves often look great with feminine outfits and sometimes even with a sweatshirt and sweatpants.

Your accessories should complement what you're wearing. They should add that extra little touch that makes an outfit memorable, exciting, and fun. I recently noticed a woman who was wearing black slacks, black boots, and a black sweater—offset by a very large ornate pair of silver and turquoise earrings. The earrings were so attention-getting that you couldn't help but notice her. The earrings really worked for her, most especially against the all-black background of her outfit. It was an awesome look and made her striking.

MAKE YOUR ACCESSORIES WORK FOR YOU

What types of accessories do you have in your closet and drawers? Go back to your Clothing Inventory in Chapter 2. What accessories did you list? You probably had all sorts of jewelry, like rings, necklaces, and bracelets. Maybe you had some scarves, a hat or two, and some earrings. Look over your comments. Did you occasionally jot a note like, "Drab. Needs some pizzazz," or "Doesn't quite work"? If a little something is missing, it just might be the right accessories.

Here are some ways you can add a touch of interest and pizzazz to your appearance.

WHY "KNOT" ADD SOME FUN WITH SCARVES

One easy, quick, and classy way to accessorize is by using scarves. Scarves can be as simple as a red paisley bandanna (the kind the cowboys might wear) or as sophisticated as a large silk rectangle with fringe. My friend Frankie Welch, of Frankie Welch Designs, has created thousands of scarves, many of which have been designed specifically for corporations, museums, and universities. She has created really interesting scarves for individuals who have commissioned her designs, including seven American presidents and their First Ladies.

Frankie, who has been a media spokesperson for the textile industry, says you're never too young to start a scarf collection. *"Look for beautiful, colorful scarves,"* Frankie advises. *"Buy them on sale, and when you're tired of wearing one, store it away. It will always be good. A classic scarf will always be in style. Look for a beautiful scarf. Designs remain the same, so even if you get tired of it for one season, you will love it a year from now. If your scarf is beginning to show wear, use it for a pocket square. You can also frame it to give color to a room."*

FOUR NIFTY WAYS TO ADD JAZZ WITH A SCARF

What are some of the things you personally can do with scarves? Here's just a short list; you can probably think of a dozen more points yourself.

- The right scarf adds color and dresses up a plain pair of jeans or slacks and a plain blouse or, sweater. A scarf can give the whole outfit a new look. Depending on the colors and fabrics, a scarf can make an outfit more sophisticated, trendy, more glamorous, and more playful.

- A scarf tied around a ponytail makes an interesting "new" hairstyle and can add a touch of color to an otherwise plain or one-colored outfit. You may want to wrap your entire head in the scarf, turban style. (A scarf can also be used on that "should have washed my hair but didn't day," whether to cover it up or pull it into a great decorated ponytail!)

- Suppose you're having one of those days where you feel blasé and no outfit looks just right. Wrap a small brightly colored scarf around your wrist, tie it in a small bow and watch all the compliments you get. It will make you feel more lighthearted and fun, and it's sure to help you lighten up!

- A scarf makes a great belt. No matter how many belts you have, there is always that one outfit for which you can't find the perfect belt. If you have a scarf in the right color, use it as a belt.

From rings to earrings, jewelry advertises your style. Some girls love large, funky pieces of jewelry. Others like dainty, delicate pieces. Some wear bracelets; others make a statement with their watches.

How about you? How has your taste in jewelry changed this year compared to last year, and why do you think it did?

_____

_____

Do you have jewelry that you haven't worn in ages? How do you decide what jewelry you no longer want to keep?

_____

_____

WHAT "STYLE" OF JEWELRY LOOKS BEST ON YOU?

How can you use jewelry to define your style and complement what you are wearing and flatter your appearance? Here are a few suggestions.

- ♦ **Use jewelry to draw attention.** I have a good friend, Maria, who nearly every day wears some different ring or bracelet. We all look forward to seeing her jewelry.

- ♦ **Be trendy.** Jewelry has fads and trends, just like everything else. Trendy jewelry doesn't have to be expensive, and it can show that you are fashionable. The clip art is cute and fun and is a good way to add a little color and style without spending much money. Don't feel like you need to follow every fad, but updating yourself now and then can be fun.

◆ **Choose jewelry that works for you.** If you are a petite girl, wearing huge jewelry can be overpowering. You don't want people to say, "The jewelry is wearing her," rather than, "She's wearing the jewelry." Experiment with different pieces in the store, looking in a mirror to see how the jewelry looks on you before buying it.

◆ **Match jewelry to your mood.** There are days when you wake up and you are in a lighthearted, fun mood. Great! Wear a silly piece of jewelry that makes everyone smile. I personally have kept some of the blue Smurf jewelry I had when I was a little girl. On days when I'm feeling totally silly, I wear a Smurf necklace. Sometimes, on those days when I'm a grouch, I wear it to remind myself to lighten up.

◆ **Do you have a nice piece that you use when you dress up?** My serious piece was a pearl ring. Whenever I wore my pearl ring, not only did I feel dressed up, it looked classy. On days when I was feeling plain, I didn't feel plain when I put it on. Maybe you have a nice piece of good jewelry, like a class ring, a gold necklace or a silver bracelet, and you wear it constantly. The good thing about a nice piece of jewelry is that it won't go out of style, you can wear it with everything, and it lasts for years.

◆ **Use jewelry to display a special interest.** The classic example of this is your class ring. You proudly wear a class ring to show your school spirit. Maybe you have a necklace from a club, or a charm bracelet with special amulets from places you've visited. Others probably ask about and you get to talk about how you acquired it, and where. Anything that you are proud of helps define who you are.

- ♦ **Make jewelry your trademark.** Your "style" of accessories defines your style and becomes a trademark of sorts. One of the first people who comes to mind for me is my friend Olanna, who is a figure skater. Every day at the rink she wears the same burgundy bodysuit brightening it up with pins. Some of the pins were silly; some were all about skating. The rest of us always kept an eye out for what pins she was wearing.

- ♦ **Use an unusual piece of jewelry as a conversation piece.** If you wear some unusual piece of jewelry, people feel like they can come up to you and comment on it, and that breaks the ice. I have a pair of silvery earrings that look like birds, and the wings flap when I move my head. They really are cute. Everyone compliments me on them and asks me where I got them. Always, it seems, wearing them leads to a conversation with someone.

SWAPPING INSTEAD OF SHOPPING: ACCESSORIES EXCHANGE

Do you have jewelry, scarves and other accessories that you hardly wear? Call your friends and schedule an accessories exchange. Ask their opinion about whether or not something looks good on you or, swap jewelry and scarves or just borrow items from each other. Sometimes you can't really tell whether you like big jewelry or smaller jewelry until you've worn the piece a couple of times.

My friend Mike bought a big, thick, heavy silver necklace. He thought it looked macho and wore it proudly—for about a day. Then he complained about how heavy the necklace was, how it caught in his clothes, and how he just couldn't stand it. I agreed to go with him to exchange the necklace. He got a lighter one and is much happier. But the point is, he had to go through all that fuss. If you borrow jewelry and accessories from your friends, you can try various pieces at home without having to put out any money.

A word to the wise: Always return the things you borrow. Not only is it unfair not to, but you can lose a good friend if you take goodwill too far. Be courteous. And be sure to specify when the item is to be returned, such as, "I need this back in 2 weeks."

And by the way, you should ask you parents if they are okay with your trading jewelry or giving your things away—especially if they paid for the piece, or bought it for you for a special occasion.

Even when it comes to accessories, it's important you know how to be a wise shopper, and the next chapter can help you become just that!

CHAPTER 6

Shopping, Shopping, Shopping, Shopping, Shopping

"I would give up shopping, but I'm not a quitter."

—ANONYMOUS

READY, SET, SHOP!

If you were going to take a final exam, you would do your homework and take the time to study, right? If you were going to run a marathon, you would prepare by training for weeks, and then stretching just before starting, right? The point is, it's wise to plan ahead for activities. Shopping (my own personal favorite activity!) also requires planning and doing your homework.

A wise shopper knows what styles and colors work best for her. She knows how to distinguish what she needs from what she wants. If you are prepared before you head out, you won't find yourself toting several bags home from the store only to realize you didn't really need the sweater you bought, or that you should have invested in a skirt to go with the sweater instead of allowing yourself to be swept off your feet by that cute little number that didn't go with anything you owned. And, what about that pair of shoes the salesperson said "would stretch," only you can't bear to wear them long enough for them to do so? Definitely not a good buy!

You can't blame yourself entirely. Everything conspires to make you spend your money. Stores know how to make their products incredibly tempting to you. Companies hire decorators who know just how to arrange the displays to catch your eye with the latest trends, and they make certain to assure you that you can't live without their goods. Everyone at the store is looking to sell you something—that's the business they are in. It's up to you to not be foolish or gullible and make the best use of your shopping time and money!

SHOP SMARTER, NOT HARDER

How can you be a smart shopper, making the best choices? As you shop, ask yourself the following questions:

1. Is it a Wise Buy?

So, there you are, walking past the store and in the window you see a very incredible jacket with a gorgeous blazing-red lining. The colors are just amazing, more dazzling than anything you've ever seen. Best of all, the jacket is marked down 35 percent.
Ten minutes later, the jacket is in your bag!
Two hours later, you're home staring at yourself in the mirror, thinking, "Why did I buy this? I already have a jacket that's a lot more practical, and besides, I'll almost never wear something this bulky."
Like many of us, you were attracted by the sales price. Sure, a good shopper should take advantage of sales, but don't let a good price seduce you into buying something you won't wear.
Remember, a sale item is no bargain if you don't have anything to wear it with in the end (especially if you're unlikely to spend the money to buy whatever else it needs in order to be a complete outfit). You may have saved $13 on that jacket, but if you never wear it, it becomes a very expensive hanger ornament in your closet! And most sale items can't be returned.

2. Is it a Good Fit?

Another question you need to ask yourself when you are thinking of buying clothing is whether it fits you well. You should be able to pinch between one and two inches of fabric around your torso, arms, and legs. Don't get into the habit of saying, "I'm always a size ten (or four, or fourteen, or whatever)." Sizes vary a lot from designer to designer, and from product to product. I have a good friend who tells me she has clothes in sizes six, eight and ten. She's a smart shopper who knows how to go for the fit rather than the size on the label. Try everything on, especially those items purchased where "all sales are final."

Don't just stand in front of the mirror admiring the beauty of the fabric and design of what you have on. Move around a little in the clothes and see how they work for you. Sleeves with seams narrower than your shoulder bones and cuffs that ride up your arm when you bend your elbow will make you look like you borrowed your little sister's clothes. Jacket sleeves should reveal about a half inch of your blouse sleeve at the wrist.

Remember to try your jackets on over your clothes, to make sure they have no pull across the back or the front when you button them. Garments that gap between the buttons or pull across the back when you reach out or fold your arms in front of you are just too small. Your jeans and slacks should break at the top of your shoes, not be so long you step on them. Pockets should stay closed, and pleats and darts should lie flat. A skirt that rides up when you sit down or pants and skirts so tight you can see panty lines are unappealing. It looks natural for a skirt to curve in a little bit, but if it hugs the hips too tightly you should go for the next larger size, or a different style.

Don't buy clothes that are too big. Sure, the baggy look can be stylish sometimes; it's a fad that comes and goes. For a while, everyone wore jeans that were so large they practically fell off their hips, and sweatshirts that could have housed a family of four! It's fun to wear the occasionally funky, fashionable outfit just to make a statement. But in the end, it's always wise to go for clothes that are comfortable.

3. Is it Easy to Care for?

Quick: Name three things you'd rather do than spend an afternoon ironing. Here's my list:

- ✔ Hangout with my friends;
- ✔ Work out;
- ✔ Go to the movie I've been waiting to see.

For most of us, ironing is not a favorite activity. Therefore, a smart shopper thinks about fabric care before she buys the item. Notice how on Sasha's Inventory she cites two items she doesn't like because of the way they look.

It just so happens that in her case, both garments are linen, a fabric that takes a lot of care. If you don't want to iron your clothing, the logical thing to do is to look for wrinkle-free clothes. You can identify fabric that won't wrinkle easily by crushing a handful of the fabric and squeezing it tightly. When you let go, notice whether the fabric stays wrinkled or smothers out easily. If the wrinkles stay in, the garment will need a lot of ironing. In addition, the piece may look wrinkled ten minutes after you've ironed it.

I hardly ever wear one of my favorite shirts because it wrinkles so quickly. I can iron it, get in the car, put on my seat belt—and within minutes my shirt is all wrinkled again. That's very frustrating! However, if something does wrinkle a little bit, don't despair. You can still avoid some ironing by taking your clothes out of the dryer (assuming they are washable and don't require dry cleaning) as soon as they are dry (or even slightly damp) and hanging them up in your closet immediately. If you leave them tossed in a heap on your bed, the wrinkles will be set in, and they'll be difficult to get out even with an iron.

Fabrics such as linen, rayon or silk wrinkle easily, whereas polished cotton, fleece or wool do not. Look back over your Clothing Inventory. Do any of the reasons for not liking an item have to do with the fabric always looking messy or unkempt?

4. Does it Need to be Dry-Cleaned Only?

And what about dry cleaning? Some clothes can't be washed but have to be dry cleaned, which can get expensive. Can you afford to have your clothes dry cleaned? Will your parents ask you to pay for the dry cleaning out of your allowance or paycheck? Dry cleaning in effect makes the price of the item higher than you originally thought. Say for example you spent $20 on a nice blouse. If you have to pay $5 or more to get it cleaned every time you wear it, in six months or so the price of the blouse has been doubled. If the blouse had cost $60 when you saw it in the store, would you have bought it in the first place? Look at the labels on the clothing and see whether they say Dry Clean Only. If they do, think really hard about whether you want to buy that item. (Of course, some things, like prom dresses or really good jackets that you wear only on special occasions, have to be dry cleaned. That's okay because you won't wear them often.)

5. Is it a Necessary Purchase?

When you go out to a buffet dinner with your folks, you probably look at all those great gooey desserts and say, "I'd like that and that and that, and I would really like that!" You all laugh, but of course you don't end up chowing down every single dessert. Just because you want something doesn't mean you need it. The same thing is true for clothing. You may want every t-shirt you see, but do you need them all?

Every time you think about buying something, stop and ask yourself, "Is it necessary? Do I really need this item, will I wear it?" If you already have five black T-shirts, do you need another black one?

If you have three denim jackets, do you need to spend money on another simply because the buttons on it are cute? One way I have learned to identify what I want, versus what I need, is through using my Clothing Inventory. This is another way you can make your Clothing Inventory work for you.

DRESSING FOR SUCCESS, NOT EXCESS

A closet of clothes that work together to bring out the best in you doesn't happen by accident. It takes work and planning to make your wardrobe all you need it to be. This is where your Clothing Inventory is useful. A Clothing Inventory can help you in three important ways:

1. **It identifies what you already have so you don't buy the same thing.** I remember my girlfriend Marcy telling me one day, *"I can't believe it. I was at the store and I spent all my money on this absolutely great belt, which I loved. Then I got home and put it on my belt rack—right next to one that was almost identical. And worst of all, it was on sale and can't be returned."* A Clothing Inventory identifies pieces you already have so you don't buy similar things.

2. **It identifies what you need.** Maybe you forgot that you spilled a cranberry smoothie on your favorite white blouse, and it won't come out. And your next favorite blouse is way too small, thanks to that recent growth spurt. You don't want to wait until five minutes before a photo session to find out you don't have the white shirt that you need for the group picture. A Clothing Inventory keeps you up to date on what things you need to replace.

3. **It identifies what you can match.** A smart shopper makes the most of her clothing dollars by buying items that work together. What good is it if you to buy that great skirt if you don't have something that works with it? When you buy something that has no "mate" (something to wear along with it), one of two things happens. Either you never wear the new piece, relegating it to the back of your closet, or you go back to the store and spend yet more money on something to match the new piece.

IT'S WHAT YOU DO WITH WHAT YOU'VE GOT

The key is to make the most of what you've got already. If you shop wisely, you should be able to create at least thirty different looks with as few as ten to fifteen pieces of clothing.

The secret is to coordinate colors to create complementary outfits using a minimum of basic pieces. This technique will save you money, time, and the headache of wondering what you're going to wear.

FOLLOWING A MASTER PLAN

Let me introduce you to the master plan. Here are the basic pieces you will need to get in order to have a wardrobe that is ample enough to take you anywhere you need to be, from hanging out with your friends, to going on a date for a special occasion, or job interviews, or school.

- **A jacket or two:** Choose a jacket in a classic style with matching buttons or no buttons at all. The fabric can be natural or a high-quality synthetic, in colors that bring out the best in you. If necessary, have it tailored (sleeves shortened or lengthened, for example) to suit your shape. If you choose a second jacket, select a complementary color for the skirts and pants you already have or intend to buy.

- **Two skirts:** Skirt lengths should best flatter your figure. One of the two should be in a color that complements your favorite jackets. For example, if you have a navy-blue jacket, you might have a matching navy-blue skirt, but also a white skirt or a camel-colored skirt.

- **Pants:** Select pants to fit your figure in a solid neutral color that goes with your jackets. Your pants should be of a quality fabric that is made well enough to handle the wear and tear of your busy life. The pants may also need to be hemmed, and you may want to leave some length of fabric to let the hem down as you grow taller.

- **Three blouses:** Every girl's wardrobe should have a simple white, off-white or ivory-colored blouse, another everyday blouse in a print or solid color with front buttons (long enough to be used as an over-blouse) and a dressier blouse in a solid color. Coordinate the colors and styles to go with your skirts, pants, and jackets.

- **Two sweaters and/or knit tops:** A cardigan sweater can work as a jacket or a blouse. Choose your other sweater or knit top with a neckline that suits you. Both sweaters should be in plain colors to complement your skirts, pants, and jackets. For summertime, a short-sleeved cotton knit is good.

- **One or two dresses:** Your first dress should have long sleeves and be in a solid color in a simple style that can be dressed up for evening wear. Select a weight appropriate for the season of the year. A second dress can be a one- or two-piece in a print or pattern. For both, choose colors that look good with your jackets.

- **Evening dress and skirt or pants:** Choose a dressy fabric (satin, brocade, or velvet, for example) for your evening clothes. It's a smart idea to select a two-piece dress for versatility and coordinate the colors so you can wear the top with your evening skirt or pants.

- **Coat:** Depending on where you live, you may need a heavy coat or just a light one. Select a neutral color that will go with everything you wear. The lines should be simple, with matching buttons. Choose a quality fabric and a style to flatter your body type.

FAD, FASHION AND "EXTREME EDGE" TRENDS

When you were going through your closet and drawers to make your Clothing Inventory, did you come across a few pieces of clothing that are so outdated they make you grimace? If you're like me, you have some clothes that you thought you absolutely couldn't live without—and now you wouldn't be seen wearing them! I have one skirt made out of fake fur in a cow pattern, white with big black blotches. I remember paying an outrageous amount of money for it (goaded on by my best friend who said, "That is so cool Jen; you must buy it!") I wore the skirt exactly once, and after the ribbing I took from wearing that gaudy thing, I then buried it in the back of my closet.

What a waste of money that was.

Obviously, clothing fads change quite often. Sure, it's fun to buy an occasional fad outfit, something wild and crazy, but you don't want a closet filled with only the latest fashions. What happens when the latest fashion becomes yesterday's news? You'll be back to staring at your closet and moaning that you have "nothing to wear"!

Choose clothes that are comfortable, and ones that fit your day-to-day activities—your lifestyle. This doesn't mean you shouldn't keep up with the style and be trendy. But before you buy that expensive pair of three-inch buffalo boots, ask yourself how often you would actually wear them. If the answer is, "once or twice," pass on the boots, even if they did look "totally cool" on your favorite rock diva. Skousers, bindis and flares that are "in" this month are sure to look unfashionable three months from now. And do you still want to be paying your mom or dad back for the money you borrowed to buy clothes you never wear?

In summary, a wise shopper (that's you!) recognizes three things:

- What styles of clothes look good on her;

- What clothing she already has and how to make the most outfits and different looks from the fewest pieces; and,

- How to spend her clothing money wisely to fill in gaps in her wardrobe and still have some money left over for fun.

MAKING YOUR WISH / WANT / NEED LIST!

You've already done the hard part of the Clothing Inventory—going through everything to decide what you have and what condition it is in. Now you get to reward yourself with the fun part of the task—listing what you need to buy.

The following chart can help you do that.

Make several copies of it, or, create it on a piece of paper.

I suggest you keep one copy in your wallet (or your mom's wallet, if she's the one paying for your clothes or has the final say in what you can buy). That way, you always have the information handy when you need it.

When you are at the store and you see that incredible sweater, you can check your list and see whether you really need it, or should you be absolutely positively certain that you have to have it, you can to consult your wish/want/need list to see what the best color is to buy.

WISH/WANT/NEED LIST

Wish/Want/Need Items	Color	Size

WISH/WANT/NEED LIST

Wish/Want/Need Items	Color	Size

CHAPTER 7

"Scents-ible" Advice: What You Should Know About Perfumes

Perfume is the unseen but unforgettable and ultimate fashion accessory.

—GABRIELLE "COCO" CHANEL

THE POWER OF FRAGRANCE

The late legendary movie actress and perfume designer Elizabeth Taylor is quoted as saying, *"Fabulous fragrances, like fabulous jewels, add mystique and confidence to every woman."* My sentiments exactly. So, when my boyfriend Derek went away to visit with family back East the summer before our senior year in high school, I was confident that his getting a periodic whiff of my perfume would keep me on his mind.

Since I couldn't be with him in person, I had to settle for writing to him every day. To make absolutely sure Derek didn't forget me, I scented all the letters and cards I mailed to him with my favorite perfume which was the perfume I wore on all our dates.

I had no doubt that when Derek smelled the scented pages, he remembered me—and our times together. I was certain it made him long to be with me again, which, of course, was just the effect I was going for! Though Derek didn't put cologne on his letters and cards to me (that's not something too many guys do, although I really don't know why), I remember his favorite cologne: Polo. To this day, if I smell a guy wearing Polo, I think of Derek.

There's no doubt that fragrance wields power over us.

I'd like to think the perfume I spritzed on my letters to Derek that summer is one of the reasons why he called me every time he received one of my letters.

Even the research proves the power of perfume. Olfactory research (the study of the effect of "smells" on people) shows that certain scents can make people feel relaxed, excited, sensual, happy, and even productive. Psychologists, for example, have found that peppermint and lily of the valley are stimulants and when these scents are sprayed in the rooms where students are taking tests, the students are more alert and score higher than when they are not used!

Because it has been discovered that certain aromas make a difference in the level of employee productivity, its been said that some Japanese firms mist certain fragrances into the air within their offices. When a jasmine fragrance is used, employees have a 21 percent drop in error rate in their work production, with lavender, a 33 percent drop, and an astounding 54 percent fewer errors with lemon wafting through the air! Other scents are valued for their relaxing properties. Researchers at New York's Sloan-Kettering Cancer Institute have found that the scent of vanilla can relax patients.

In short, scents have influence.

THE RULE: THE EARLIER THE HOUR, THE LIGHTER THE SCENT

The rule is, the earlier the hour, the lighter the scent. Because scent has such a powerful influence, you have to be considerate how you use it. Perfume can make others enjoy being around you or run for cover when they can smell you five minutes before you arrive. And no, wearing perfume (or cologne or aftershave) is not a substitute for taking a bath. Use scent to enhance, not to disguise.

A lot of people have the mistaken idea that "if a little bit is good, more is great." Colleen, a classmate of mine, doused herself with her favorite musk-scented perfume every day. I could hardly handle being in the same room as her. Sitting next to Colleen for even twenty minutes would give me a headache.

When Colleen left the room, her perfume remained behind for what seemed like hours. It was never hard to find where Colleen was or had been in school—you just followed your nose. Now, it wasn't that the perfume smelled bad or anything, it was actually very nice. The problem was overkill because Colleen was using way too much.

If the students in your classroom pass out when you're around, you know you've doused yourself too much!

A word of warning: Perfume can stain your clothing, so don't douse your wardrobe.

PULSE POINTS: WHERE TO WEAR PERFUME

How do you know how much to put on and where? International perfume expert Jan Moran (and author of *Fabulous Fragrances*, a wonderful book about all perfumes, says that one dab of perfume should be applied on the pulse points. A pulse point is a part of your body where your pulse is strong. Each time your heart beats, or the pulse throbs, a little bit of scent is released. Good places are behind each ear, and on each wrist and at the bend in elbows and knees and in the hollow of your throat. Some people like to spray a little mist on their necks. Again, if you're in close quarters, like the classroom or a movie theater, go easy.

My friend Kiley has really beautiful hair, which her boyfriend loves to touch. Naturally, she spritzes a little perfume on top of her hair. And Selena, another friend of mine, likes to smell her own perfume and so she puts a dab on her hands. When she is not wearing perfume, she uses scented hand lotion made from the same perfume.

You maybe don't notice how much perfume you are wearing, but others can! This is because of sensory adaptation, meaning you get used to a smell when you are around it a lot. I have two kitties and am very meticulous about keeping their litter box clean. But the other day, when a friend was visiting, she walked into my house and remarked, "Jennifer, you need to clean out the kitty box!" I can no longer smell my kitties—but others can!

The same adaptation happens with perfume. When you've been wearing the perfume for a while (sometimes for only a minute or two), you don't smell it anymore. Some time back, my mother and I were in New Orleans at the American Library Association doing a book signing. All of a sudden, the air was filled with a glorious scent of perfume. My mother looked up and said, "Oh, someone smells simply wonderful!" At her saying this, the woman first in line looked around to see if she could detect the scent my mom was smelling. "I don't smell anything," she said.

My mother and I looked at each other and naturally had to laugh because the woman looking around was the woman wearing the glorious-smelling perfume. But she was so used to wearing it that she could no longer smell it!

"What are you wearing?" my mother asked the woman.

"Giorgio," the woman replied.

"Oh, it's one of my favorites!" my mom told her. "I love the floral scents!"

"Me, too," the woman said. "I've been wearing it for I don't how many years. Whenever my husband doesn't know what else to get me for a gift, he gives me perfume. I now must have 3 bottles, so I'll be wearing it for a long time!"

The problem with getting used to the perfume is that you put it on and think that the fragrance isn't strong enough—so you dab on some more.

Suggestion: If you are used to your perfume and are considering adding more, ask your friends. The scent may already be strong enough. A simple, "Do you like the smell of my perfume," or, "Can you smell the perfume I'm wearing?" will get you the information you need to know.

BODY CHEMISTRY AND PERFUME: HOW TO BE "SCENT-SATIONAL"

Have you noticed that the exact same perfume or cologne can smell one way on one person and either subtly or entirely different on another person? This is because each of us has her own individual body chemistry, which can interact differently with the ingredients in any given perfume. My mother has a favorite scent and to me, the smell of her perfume is simply glorious. Every now and then when we are traveling together, I'll ask her if I can use her perfume. She always says yes—and always, no one compliments me on how I smell when I wear it. But they do compliment me on my own perfume!

Perhaps a cologne you admire on a friend doesn't smell as good on you. Or your favorite perfume seems different in Winter than in Summer, different still when you're happy or upset. Those differences aren't imaginary; weather, body chemistry and even mood can affect fragrance. Your mood and the temperature outside all affect how a fragrance smells on you, too.

You may even notice a change in the way your favorite fragrances smell on you if you've changed your diet, if you're taking a new medication, if you're under more stress than usual or are menstruating.

Here are some other interesting facts about perfume:

- People with a higher proportion of body fat retain scent longer.
- People with oily or darker skin retain a scent longer than those with dry or paler skin.
- Fragrance evaporates more quickly during exercise, or if your skin is dry, or if you are on a low-fat diet, or if you live in a cold climate.
- Your body emits more of the perfume you are wearing when you perspire or spend time in warm temperatures.
- The sun spoils the oils in perfume and changes the way it smells. If you carry perfume in your purse and know that heat can alter your fragrance.
- Experts say it is a good idea to store expensive perfumes in your refrigerator. If you do this, place it in a plastic bag or else other foods in the refrigerator will smell like your perfume!
- At home, store your fragrance bottles away from direct sunlight and extreme heat. You might put it in a drawer or beneath the sink in your bathroom.

COORDINATE YOUR PERFUME WITH THE SEASON

Did you know that King Louis XV loved the smell of fragrances so much that he demanded that his court wear a different perfume for every day of the week? Fragrance experts say there is no such thing as one perfume that fits all people, or each person all year long. You already know that you use scents to match your mood but there's another commonsense consideration in deciding what perfume to wear: What season is it?

Experts recommend you select a heady floral or an oriental fragrance in the Winter; in the summer (or if you live year-round in a warm climate) select a lighter floral or citrus scent. The goal is to choose a soft light cologne or an eau de toilette. On a crisp fall day, try chypres (a warm sweet smell of oakmoss or a woody scent) because it best matches the mood and "feel" of the season. When spring returns after a long winter, go with a "green" perfume—these smell clean and fresh, and match everyone's mood for a season that the late great Robin Williams so aptly epitomized when he said, "Springtime is nature's way of saying 'Let's boogie.'"

With all this information, do you find yourself thinking that wearing a perfume shouldn't be all that complicated? It may sound complicated, but it's not.

Once you understand even the basics about the six different categories of scents, your idea about perfume will change forever.

The next section explains the essence of understanding the six different styles of scents. Don't forget to teach your boyfriend this information. If you do, and if he's a guy who likes to give his girl perfume for her birthday, chances are he'll give you a perfume in the "category" of scents that works best with your body chemistry.

And here's another way to use this information: When someone (like Mom, Dad or your grandparents) asks you what you want for a birthday, add perfume to your list—especially scents that you love but can't afford to buy for yourself just yet!

TOP NOTES, HEART NOTES, BASE NOTES: 6 STYLES OF SCENT

There are a few basic categories of scents. Each of these is as different from the next one as one primary color is from another. Each category is based on the main theme of the scent, for example, floral or spicy. When you get an idea which division of scent works best on you, you can narrow your search down to colognes in that division and avoid wasting money on scents that wind up unused in a drawer, only to be tossed out a year later.

- 👍 **Floral fragrances** are the largest category of scents. Many are made up of single flower scents although more are being created with flowers such as rose, gardenia, carnation; jasmine, honeysuckle, and hyacinth. Floral scents are fresh, soft, and sensual and make you smell like what else—a flower! Popular fragrances include Joy, Giorgio, Chloe, DKNY L'Air du Temps, White Diamonds, Champs-Elysees, Amarige, Escada, Calyx and 273. Florals have a springtime and cool, summer-day smell—one I grew up around; my mother is a Spring.

- 👍 **Oriental fragrances** are heavier, richer, and spicier scents. They are made up of exotic resins such as incense, musk, and spices. These scents are often considered ideal for cool weather and evening wear. Classic examples of perfumes with this kind of scent are Shalimar, Opium, Angel, Guess? and Obsession. Winter girls love Oriental fragrances because they smell so divine on them.

- 👍 **Chypres** (pronounced "sheep-ra") is French for cyprus. Chypres scents have a warm and sweet smell are often described as woody-mossy. They're created from earthy substances such as oakmoss and sandalwood. Classic chypres scents are Versace, Paloma Picasso, Y, Ysatis, and V'E Versace. I love to wear Versace in the fall to beach parties. That mossy smell works perfectly with a mohair sweater worn around a crackling fire. I'm an Autumn girl, and my favorite perfume of all is Cartier—another chypres scent.

- 👍 **Green scents** are those that bring to mmd the fragrance of a freshly mowed lawn or a walk in a forest—pine, juniper, sage. It's a real summer scent. If you are a Summer girl, probably you find your-self adoring scents in this category. Classic examples of green scents include Di Borghese, Aliage, Pheromone and Tommy Hilfiger's Freedom for Her.
- 👍 **Cypress scents** are those fresh, share, clean fragrances that provoke thoughts of citrus fruits, such as tangerine, lemon, orange, grapefruit, and lime. While they are often thought to be mostly men's fragrances, classic examples of their use in women's perfumes can be found in Eau de Herm, Diorella, Eau de Patou and Eau de Guerlain.
- 👍 **Fougere** (meaning fern in French, pronounced "foozh-air," is an interpretation of fresh green ferns, with a hint of lavender, citrus and oakmoss. Fougere ingredients are most often used in many of the "his and her" fragrances. E Green Fougere by Clive, Fogg Unisex, Fougère Mania Eau de Toilette are a few that young people enjoy.

Each of these scents are further broken down into classifications. I won't elaborate on each one here, but should you be interested knowing more, you can Google it or ask a salesclerk at the perfume counter for a profile of fragrances by scent type.

Knowing all about perfume is their business, and it's been my experience that they sincerely want you to find a perfume you'll enjoy.

Sub-classifications of Perfumes

Florals	green, fruity, fresh, aldehyde, amber and oriental
Oriental	amber, spice
Chypres	fruity, floral—animalistic, floral, fresh, and green
Citrus	none other
Fougere	none other

What perfume belongs where is determined according to its ingredients. To help manufacturers come up with a new scent, and to help buyers know what is in a perfume, each fragrance is further divided into "Notes" according to dominant ingredients. The most potent ingredients, the ones setting tone for the fragrance, are called top notes. The secondary ingredient(s) are called base notes. Let's take Bijan for an example:

Top Note	ylang-ylang, narcissus, orange blossom
Heart Note	Persian jasmine, Bulgarian rose, lily of the valley
Base Note	Moroccan oakmoss, sandalwood, patchouli

When you factor this information in, then what you can decide is not just if you are a floral, but rather floral-oriental. If you are, then scents like Bijan are exactly the scent you want.

Whew! Never knew there was so much to just smelling good, did you? If you find all this fascinating, you aren't alone. When I explain it to others, they are amazed at how they already know this information on working level; knowing why affirms what they have already experienced.

This knowledge can serve you well in other ways. I once bought a bottle of perfume simply because it smelled incredibly wonderful on the clerk at fragrance bar in a department store. That's not such a good idea. After making the purchase, I spritzed it on and then continued shopping. Within an hour I had a real headache—and got one every time I wore that perfume!

Nor is it a good idea to buy a perfume because of a real cool bottle, or a glamorous ad announces the latest and hottest trend and promises. Fashion is fun but let your nose be the authority on what scent is right for you regardless of the trend. Select what is best for you and most appropriate for the occasion.

So how should you buy perfume? The following section can help you make the right choice.

THE NOSE KNOWS: THE THREE LEVELS OF A PERFUME'S FRAGRANCE

Just because you like a first whiff at the fragrance bar in the store doesn't mean that you'll appreciate the scent when you take it home. That's because scent changes over time. A fragrance has three distinct levels.

- 👍 **The first level of a perfume can last from thirty seconds to three minutes.** While a fragrance is usually purchased based on the impression this level gives, this isn't necessarily how you will be smelling hours later.
- 👍 **After the first level of scent wears off, you enter level two.** This middle-level fragrance lasts up to ten minutes. If you put on perfume a few minutes before your date arrives, you are at the second level of the scent by the time you go to greet him.
- 👍 **Level three of a fragrance is called the "dry down."** This scent is what you smell several hours after you apply the scent. This is the main level of the scent, the level that lasts the longest. Therefore, it is wise to wear a scent twenty minutes or more before you buy it. Since the aroma will be going through these different levels, you'll need time to know whether or not you really like the way it smells on you over time.

Perfume expert Jan Moran says it's not a good idea to try on more than three fragrances at a time in the store when you are trying to find one you like. Why? Because your nose gets overwhelmed and you really won't be able to decipher the difference between the scents.

So, as you can see, when it comes to selecting a cologne or perfume, impulse shopping is not a great idea. Try a fragrance, and an hour later, see if you still like the way it smells.

As time passes, your body chemistry also changes as you change your activities. For example, in the morning you may be sitting in your biology class but by the afternoon you are in gym class doing just five more crunches trying to top your personal record. A scent that worked well when you were sitting still in the morning may not work so well when you are huffing and puffing in the afternoon. Therefore, it's a good idea to take home samples when they are available. That way, you can have more than one trial run for smelling the scent, wearing it in different settings.

This also gives you a chance to see if the scent is right for you in other ways. For instance, does wearing it for a long time give you a headache? Remember how I mentioned earlier that my friend Colleen's musk gave me a headache when I was around her? Even the nicest scent, your favorite one that you love wearing, can be too much after a few hours.

When you try a certain perfume, keep reapplying it every few hours for a day and keep track of whether you have any reaction. Do you feel slightly dizzy or nauseated? Are you getting a little pink rash where you applied the perfume?

Each of us has a unique body chemistry. Not all categories of scents will work with your body.

BUYING SCENTS WITH SENSE

How much should you pay for great smells? It depends on your budget. But you may need to shop around. You can find some wonderful bargains on good perfumes in discount stores, chain stores, and drugstores. There are also a number of "designer" fragrances that are far less expensive than real perfumes. These are generally imitation or scented oil. Designer fragrances can be good for regular school days and activities, but as a rule, their fragrance doesn't last as long as cologne or true perfume.

How much should you spend on perfumes? It depends.

The more fragrance oils used in a formula, the longer the fragrance will last—and the higher the retail price will be. Parfum (or perfume, they mean the same thing) is the most intense form of fragrance and can be pricey.

This is followed by eau de parfum, eau de toilette and eau de cologne. These last two terms, eau de toilette and cologne, are virtually interchangeable.

Consider trying eau de toilette, especially if you haven't worn a particular scent you are thinking about buying. Even though it is not as intense as the stronger version of it will be, the eau de toilette is a good way to test it before you invest a lot of money, and until you're sure you like the way it smells on you.

The difference between perfume and eau de toilette is that a perfume is made with natural and expensive oils, which, being heavier, hold the scent of the perfume much longer than an eau de toilette—which is made with less expensive ingredients, such as alcohol and other substances.

An eau de toilette is therefore much cheaper ounce by ounce, but once you have it on, it will wear off at a fraction of the time that perfume would.

So do your homework on the various scents including aromas. The goal is to find those that are just right for you!

THE AROMA OF YOUR HOME: SCENTS IN YOUR HOUSE

Have you ever heard of *"aromatherapy"*? You know that *aroma* means scent. *Therapy* is healing, curing, or treating.

Aromatherapy can help you feel better. Think about how often this happens to you. You walk in the house, tired after a long day of school. But wait! Is that fresh baked chocolate-chip cookies you smell? That great aroma makes you start grinning as you dash to the cookie jar, and your mood is better even before you take the first bite! That's the idea: a scent can have an impact on you so go for "positive" impact.

Maybe you enter a room that has just been cleaned with a pine cleaner, and you enjoy the "outdoors" smell. Do you (or your parents or friends) use a scented refresher in the car? I use one that smells like strawberries, because I love the smell of them. One friend uses a car deodorizer that gives off the same smell as a brand-new car.

Aromatherapy is nothing new. For hundreds of years people have used scents and essential oils taken from herbs and flowers to treat headaches and depression, to relieve stress and to improve memory. The use of scent has been shown to create greater physical and emotional health. If you're going through a lot of stress and need a pick-me-up, why not try an aromatherapy designed to be calming?

Here are some ways you can use scents to make yourself happier and maybe even healthier.

- ✔ *Use potpourri.* Potpourri is a mixture of dried flowers and spices. It often comes in a bowl and can be found in all sorts of scents from heavy and musky to light and floral. I keep a dish of light potpourri right by my bed. When I swish the flowers around, the scent renews itself. The scent helps me to relax and sleep better.

Here's a Tip: As the roses in your garden (or from that special someone) begin to fade, pick off the petals and put them in a bowl or linen pouch and spray them with perfume.

- ✔ *Burn scented candles.* Candles are very inexpensive, much less expensive, in general, than perfumes or colognes) so you can use a lot of them, especially while soaking in a bubble bath! Caution! Don't fall asleep with the lighted candle burning. You don't want to end up burning your house down.

- ✔ *Scent your drawers and closets.* You can find sachets (little scented pillows of cloth, usually no larger than a few square inches) in all sorts of scents. You can even make your own by dribbling a couple of drops of your favorite cologne on a piece of cloth. If your perfume bottle is empty, don't throw it away, open it up and put it in your drawer. There is enough scent left to make your clothes smell great. You can also rub a little perfume oil directly on the wood inside your drawer.

- ✔ *Use fragrance on your pillows and sheets.* It's so great to go to bed at night with sheets and pillows that smell of your favorite scent. But as alway, see how this works for you. If for example, your begin to get headaches, then stop using the scent to see if it also stops your headache. And of course, be sure to let your parents in on what you're doing. They will need to know how you're feeling, and doing.

www.ingramcontent.com/pod-product-compliance
Lightning Source LLC
Chambersburg PA
CBHW020808160426
43192CB00006B/493